Lord, Could You Hurry a Little?

RUTH HARMS CALKIN

LIVING BOOKS
Tyndale House Publishers, Inc.
Wheaton, Illinois

Tenth printing, April 1988

Library of Congress Catalog Card Number 82-74409
ISBN 0-8423-3816-0
Copyright © 1983 by Ruth Harms Calkin
Printed in the United States of America

To

ISABEL ANDERS

My very capable editor

My caring friend

Always with me

From start to finish!

CONTENTS

Your Home,
My Heart

BE THOU EXALTED

"Be thou exalted, Lord
In thine own strength;
So will we sing
And praise thy power."

Yes, Lord, Yes!
David's prayer is my prayer.

Be exalted in my day-by-day agenda
In my motives and dreams
My priorities and goals.
Even in my failures, Lord
As You turn them into stepping stones
Toward spiritual growth.
Be exalted in my worship and praise
In my sobbing and singing.
Be exalted in my secret thoughts
My emotional responses.
Be exalted in my daily routine
The delays, the unexpected emergencies
The disappointments that often come.
Lord God, as You are exalted
In heaven and on earth
Be exalted in Your home—my heart.

THE MOST—THE LEAST

Lord, when I feel exuberant
Bursting with energy and strength
When everything in my life
Seems to be going amazingly well
Then, dear God
I think I can accomplish anything for You.
In fact, *everything*.
I'm ready to go for it!
But when pain and depression grab me
And trials clobber me unmercifully
When I am hurt by criticism
Or neglected by my family
Or burdened with numerous demands
Then I am convinced
I can serve You in no way at all.

Often, dear child
When you think
You are doing the most
You are serving the least.
And when you think
You are doing the least
As you rest in my love
You are serving Me best.

BACKBITING

Dear Lord, I am troubled
By what I read this morning.
The Psalmist David asked
"Lord, who shall abide in thy tabernacle?"
Part of the answer is—
"He that backbiteth not with his tongue."
O God, keep me from yielding
To the slanderous temptation
That so often trips me up.
May I bite my own tongue
Before backbiting others.

ASK ME ANYTHING

I have to say it, Lord—
I just have to say it:
Sometimes You seem to be
Extremely inquisitive.
In orderly sequence You ask . . .
How are you spending your time?
What are your spiritual goals?
Why do you harbor secret resentment?
Where are you growing in depth?
When will you put Me first?
Lord, is nothing personal or private
In my day-by-day living?
Must I continually expose my heart?
Are You forever the "Hound of Heaven"
Seeking me out
Searching, sorting, pointing?

Child of my constant concern
If I withdrew from you
Leaving you totally alone
Would you be pleased?

O dear God
No, no!
Ask me anything—
Anything at all
But never let me go!

THAT LITTLE

O dear God
There is within me
A deep, intense longing
To use whatever gifts
You've entrusted to me.
But, Lord, they seem so small.
There's so little I can do
So little I can say.

My timid child
It is just "that little"
That I ask from you.
Hear what I say:
OBEY!

A DOUBT

Sometimes, dear Lord
You don't seem
To love me at all.

Sometimes, dear child
You seem to ignore
The eternal facts.

THE DIFFERENCE

O dear God
Help me to grow
More like You
In spite of my circumstances.

Wounded child
You will grow
More like Me
Because of your circumstances.

THE EXCHANGE

O God
You are continually
Stripping me . . .
Stripping me . . .
Of all my natural plans
My dreams
My successes
My secret ambitions.
For so long, Lord
My natural achievements
Have been my one consuming thought.
And now they lie before me
In a paltry heap.
God, why?

My child
It is the only way
I can begin to shower you
With all the joys
Of the supernatural.
Do you resist that exchange?

WRONG CENTER

Lord, I'm so discouraged.
Again and again I've struggled
To get hold of myself
But I simply can't do it.

Weary child
Your center is wrong.
The secret is—
Get hold of Me.

THE ANSWER

Lord, I can't do it!
I can't do it!
I can't do it!

My child
I have appointed you.

INTRUSIONS

A thousand intrusions
Have crowded in on my life today.
My reaction, Lord?
I've resented every one.
And now I read in Your Word
That I'm to put out the welcome sign!
In fact, I must welcome each intrusion
As a personal friend.
(Perhaps even serve tea, Lord?)
You assure me that You have a purpose
For their continual persistence:
My faith needs depth
My endurance needs development.

I have no argument with that, Lord
But I had hoped that an hour or two
Of trial and testing would suffice.
Or a day at most, dear God.
But again You remind me
That the process must continue
Until maturity becomes my password
And independence becomes my goal
And the Crown of Life becomes my reward.

PRIORITIES

O God
I desperately need Your wisdom
In determining my priorities.
When I fail to make my own choices
Under Your personal guidance
Everybody else chooses for me.
Then what happens?
I become a jagged, jittery Martha.
Singleness of mind and heart—
This is my urgent need.
Lord, I know there is time
For all You want me to do
But somehow I have not yet learned
To acknowledge my own limitations.
Teach me to say *yes* less hurriedly
And *no* more prayerfully.

BOTH

Lord
I'm so excited
So elated
So joyfully overwhelmed
At the amazing answer to prayer
You've flung into my outstretched arms
I don't know whether to laugh or cry.
If You don't mind
I think I'll do both.

LONGING HEART

It's raining today.
The rain is gentle but persistent.
Lord, I quietly wait
With Your Book open before me
Wondering what new insights I will acquire.
How will You satisfy my longing heart?

One by one the raindrops touch each other
Whispering their own private secrets
Before touching the ground.
Dear God, Creator of falling rain
As I saturate myself in Your Word
Whisper Your secrets to my thirsty soul.

THE TIME IS NOW

O God
No temptation is irresistible.
I can absolutely trust You
To keep the temptation
From becoming so strong
That I can't stand against it.
You've promised this
And You will do what you say.
But I don't need the promise
For yesterday or tomorrow, Lord.
I need it today. Desperately.
This very moment.

DON'T STOP, LORD

Lord
In asking You
To make me whole
I certainly didn't know
What I was in for.
You have ransacked me
Until I sometimes feel
There is nothing left.
But don't stop, Lord
Please don't stop!
I'm trusting that the product
Will be worth the process.

QUANDARY

In the corner of our kitchen
There's a spider.
He knows he shouldn't be there
But with all the boldness he possesses
He sings his spider-song.
O dear God
Creator of all things
How do I tell a spider he doesn't belong?

PROCRASTINATION

Lord, I am determined
To avoid procrastination
Like the plague.
I refuse to squander the valuable hours
You've generously entrusted to me.
For too long I've endured
The torture of agonizing guilt
When I close my eyes and ears
To obvious tasks and responsibilities.
I'm weary of obeying the clamoring voice
"Come on, do it tomorrow."

The letters stacked high on my desk . . .
The calls I promised to make . . .
The closets that need organizing . . .
Tomorrow.
The ironing stuffed in the basket . . .
The book I must return to a friend . . .
The pounds I must lose . . .
Tomorrow.
The habit forms.
Tomorrow . . . tomorrow . . . tomorrow . . .
No way out?
Yes, Lord, You assure me there is.
A sacred resolution
Backed by Your infinite power.
Then two declarations
Day after day:
One: *I will not put it off.*
Two: *I will do it now.*

GREEN LIGHT

Thank You, dear Lord
That I need never
Push through jumbled traffic
Or maneuver around sudden detours
To get to Your Throne Room.
All the signal lights are green.

FREE ME COMPLETELY

O dear God
This aching desire!
My heart cries for it
Longs for it
With deep, throbbing intensity!
Yet in the depths of my soul
I know that what I ask
Is not Your highest
Or Your best for me.
I cannot come to You boldly
Nor can I make my request
In the Name of Your Son.
I dare not ask for a stone
When You offer me bread.
And so, my Lord
Though the longing clutches my heart
I yield it to You totally.
I ask not that You grant my desire
But that You free me completely
From desiring it.

WHAT IS YOUR SCHEDULE, GOD?

Lord
Many years ago Martin Luther said
"It is God's nature
To make something out of nothing.
That is why God cannot make anything
Out of him who is not yet nothing."

In ways I had never anticipated, Lord
Slowly but persistently
You continue Your hammering and crushing
In every hidden crevice of my life.
You seem determined
To reduce me to nothing
In order to make me something.
I wonder . . .
What is Your schedule, God?
As You creatively continue
To reshape and remake me
How long will the process last?
Lord, could You hurry a little?

PATIENCE

Lord, as I read Your Word today
I underlined these words:
"Don't be impatient for the Lord to act.
Keep traveling steadily along his pathway
And in due season he will honor you
With every blessing."
I know I need more patience, Lord
But I simply cannot create it.
I plead with You to do it for me.
And, Lord, could You hurry a little?

COULD YOU HURRY A LITTLE

Lord, I know there are countless times
When I must wait patiently for You.
Waiting develops endurance.
It strengthens my faith
And deepens my dependence upon You.
I know You are Sovereign God—
Not an errand boy
Responding to the snap of my finger.
I know Your timing is neatly wrapped
In Your incomparable wisdom.
But, Lord
You have appointed prayer
To obtain answers!
Even David the Psalmist cried
With confident boldness:
"It is time, O Lord, for you to act."
God, on this silent sunless morning
When I am hedged in on every side
I too cry boldly.
You are my Father, and I am Your child.
So, Lord, could You hurry a little?

ONLY GOODNESS

What glorious words of wonder
Come from the Apostle Peter.
He wrote, "But we are looking forward
To God's promise of new heavens
And a new earth afterwards
Where there will be only goodness."

O dear God
"Where there will be only goodness."
After centuries of war, greed, and lust
After indulgences shamelessly practiced
After hatred, hostility
Jealousy and abuse.
Murder and martyrdom
Crime and cruelty
Curses and rebellion.
After whimpering cries from starving children
After tragedy and catastrophe
Loneliness and despair
At last . . . at long last
"There will be only goodness."
O dear Lord
Your promise is Your guarantee
But please hurry a little!

I WONDER WHY?

Lord, again and again
I've been grimly aware
That when You want to
Reveal deep secrets
Or when You want to unlock new doors
To show me something wonderful
You always first take me
Through a time
Of narrowing horizons
And ominous darkness.

O God
I wonder why?

THREE MISERABLE DAYS

Lord
For three miserable days now
I have stubbornly resisted You.
I've balked and argued
I've looked for possible detours
I've shouted outrageous excuses
And I've tried in every possible way
To sidestep You.
All of this, only to discover
That my clenched-fist resistance
Has been far more unbearable
Than the obedience You required of me.
Lord, may I please have another chance?

NOT TOMORROW

Lord
You have promised forgiveness
To my sincere repentance.
With all my heart
I praise You for that.
But may I never reject
The unalterable truth
That You have not promised tomorrow
To my procrastination.

TOO OFTEN

Dear, dear Lord
Too often in my life
I've messed around
In my tiny dirt plots
When through Your glorious power
I could have moved mountains.
Please change me!

PRAISE UPON PRAISE

O Father
Through the years
You have permitted
Hurt upon hurt
In my God-planned life.
This early morning
Even before I greet the dawn
I offer You
Praise upon praise
For You are transforming every hurt
Into a holy hallmark—
A genuine guarantee
Of my permanent identification
With You.

THE ADVERSARY

The Adversary!
How crafty, how clever his tactics.
Sometimes he comes as a roaring lion
Attempting to tear me
Into scattered bits.
At other times he comes
As an angel of light
Suggesting with coy subtlety
"How could anything so beautiful be wrong?"
Lord, I stand clad in Your armor
Claiming Your Name
And singing Your praise
For Your power over him
Is greater by far
Than his power over me.

THIS WEDNESDAY MORNING

O dear God
In Your Word You tell me most pointedly
That I must love my enemies—
That I must pray for those
Who despitefully use me.
I see there is no escape
If I am serious in my intent to obey You.
Beginning today, dear God
Though my heart still bleeds
I have set my will to obey.
By the gift of Your grace
I choose to saturate with love
The one who deliberately wounded me.
But it must be Your love, Lord.
You know I cannot manufacture my own.

So on this Wednesday morning
Five minutes past ten o'clock
I make the deliberate choice
To pray sincerely for the one
Whose act of betrayal has left my heart
A leaden weight.
And tomorrow, Lord?
And then tomorrow?
I shall continue to depend upon You
Until all the exits of my heart are open
And forgiveness pours in like Niagara Falls.

THANK YOU, LORD

Lord, all day long
I have dashed frantically
From one pressing task to another
Without giving a single thought
To a wise and workable plan of action.
I started a dozen projects
And finished none.
In my frenzied effort
To save minutes
I have squandered hours.
Because of my inefficiency
Some things I should have done
Will now never be done.

In my carelessness I broke things.
I stormed and shouted.
Without a chuckle or a smile
I quarreled with myself
From morning until evening.
Now, haunted by my own failure
My energies are drained
And my nerves are strung tight.

Lord, I know I am accountable to You
For the management of my time.
I cringe to think of it.
But right now
I know nothing to do
But wait before You.

I know You are a forgiving Lord—
A merciful, loving Father.

If You will give me
A new shining tomorrow
I will unwrap it with gratitude and joy.
I will depend upon You to guide me
In sorting my priorities.
Hour by hour I will reflect
Upon Your clear promise:
"I will instruct you and teach you . . .
I will guide you with my eye."

Thank You, Lord!

INCONSISTENCY

Lord, forgive me
For telling You
I love You
When deep in my heart
I frantically fight
Against Your Will.

GRIEF

Lord, You who permit my grief
Are the only One
Who can assuage it.
I wonder—
Do you permit grief
That I might learn
To be content
With nothing less
Than the comfort of God?
Whatever the reason
One thing I am learning:
You make useful to me
All that You permit.
So, dear God
Though a great ache
Wells within my heart
I ask You to grip my life.
Empower me to go
From depth to depth with You
Until I am a "wounded healer"
Bringing Your comfort to others
As You are now comforting me.

As a
Little Child

IT'S FOR KEEPS

Lord
Even when I came to You
As a little child
Not quite nine years old
You knew the worst, the very worst
About each future sin and failure.
Still You accepted me
With Your arms wide open.
You held me close to Your loving heart
And whispered, "It's for keeps!"
Had I been an adult
You might have captured my attention
With Your cry from the Cross:
"It is finished."
But You whispered to a little girl
Who understood perfectly, "It's for keeps."

O Lord
I praise You for the liberating fact
That through all the passing years
I have never had to produce or perform
To guarantee my position in You.
It is You, not I, who maintains my status.
Nobody, NOBODY can produce an ounce of
    evidence
To cause You to change Your mind.
Year after year, day by day
Your words still ring in my heart:
"It's for keeps!"

YOUR GUARANTEE

Ten years old.
Red hair, blue eyes.
One huge freckle
In the middle of his nose.
Blue-striped T-shirt.
Bubble gum in his pocket.
Most frequent complaint
"I'm hungry."
His turn to say grace
At the dinner table:

"Dear God
Thank You for the meatloaf
And salad and bread
And all the other stuff.
And God
Please don't ever
Let anything happen to You
Or we're all sunk. Amen."

Just time for a catch-breath:
"Please pass the bread."

Lord, nothing is ever
Going to happen to You!
From everlasting
To everlasting
You are God . . .
So we need not fear

Even if the world blows up
And the mountains
Crumble into the sea.
Your own Word
Is Your guarantee.

THE STORY

Lord, I love the story
The young mother told me.
Through it You spoke to me . . .

The morning was loaded
With little-boy questions.
Questions poppin' from every direction:

"Is God everywhere, Mom?"
"Yes, Kevin, He is."

"Is God here in our kitchen?"
"Of course, honey."
"Can He smell the cookies you baked?"
"I'm sure He can."

"Are you going to give Him one?"
"I'm going to give *you* one, Kevin.
If you sit on the stool
You may have one right now."

"Wow, Mom, the cookies are great!"

"Kevin, why are you sitting so close
To the edge of the stool?
I'm afraid you'll fall off."

"No I won't, Mom.
I just moved over to make room for God.
If I fall He'll pick me up."

Lord, Kevin was right.
Your own Word affirms it:

"If they fall, they will not stay down
Because the Lord will help them up."

Thank You for my two special friends—
Kevin and his mother.

LOOK OUT

All during summer vacation
I hear my nervous neighbor
Call a warning to her children.
With obvious anxiety she shouts
"Look out, look out!"

Lord, if only she would learn
To trust and look up
Perhaps she would be less concerned
That her children look out.

THE INFALLIBLE TEST

Lord
Often I have wondered
If my love for You is genuine.
Or do I flippantly mouth it
Like a small child
Saying grace at the table?
But today as I read Your Word
I discovered the one infallible test:
"The one who obeys me
Is the one who loves me."
Lord, never again need I wonder.
You have made it plain enough.

THE NEXT THING

O Lord
I love what You said to me
In Your Word today:
*"In the place
Where you have walked in defeat
There will I cause victory
To break forth."*

Father, I look to You
To do that very thing.
You will not let me
Be ultimately defeated.
And when the battle is won
I must confidently ask
What is the next thing?

IT'S BOUND TO BE GOOD

When I was ten
I thought seriously about death only once.
My grandmother had died.
When my father came home from her service
He gathered us into his arms
And said with soft tenderness
"Just think—now your daddy is an orphan."
My grief for my father far exceeded
Whatever grief I felt about my grandmother.
She was in heaven, she could see again.
Throwing my arms around my father
I sobbed with sympathy
"Daddy, we'll take care of you!"

When I was twenty the reality of death
Left its deep, ugly wound
The day a strapping college student
Fell dead on our college football field.

At thirty I was too busy to count years.
I spent most of my time counting
Missing buttons, unmatched socks
Spots on carpeting, calendar dates.
Once in awhile I counted calories.

When I was fifty my beloved parents died
Within five months of each other.
I sobbed and rebelled
I sobbed and grieved
Finally I sobbed and relinquished them.

The years pass so swiftly.
One of these days, without any doubt
Jesus will be coming, and I will be going.
All my cherished possessions will remain.
I'll take nothing with me
But an overwhelming abundance of love.
At times I think of it wonderingly
When I lie in the quiet stillness.

Only once did I awaken my husband.
I needed his gentle assurance.
I remember that he said
"It will happen to us both, my darling.
But one thing we know—
Jesus will be there, so it's bound to be good."

I'm not counting years, I'm *living* them.
Through all Eternity I'll go right on *living*.
One thing I know, dear Lord:
You'll be there, so it's bound to be good!

HELP ME TO GROW UP

O God
A little child
Hugging a blue-eyed doll
Is a precious picture.
But Lord
I am a grown woman
Too often hugging trinkets
When I ought to be
Hugging a needy world.
Lord, help me to grow up!

SLOW WALK

I remember how it was in my family
Before I was married . . .

My brothers emptied the trash.
I dusted the furniture.
There was no particular Scripture
To support the division of tasks
But we accepted its finality.

When I stood in my own small kitchen
Glaring defiantly at the overflowing basket
The harassing thought kept twirling:
Husbands empty wastebaskets
And wives dust furniture.

But who said so?
I have two arms and two legs.
I know the exact route to the trash can.
Suddenly I remembered the many times
My husband dried the dishes for me.
So I hummed a flimsy little tune
And emptied the basket—painlessly.

O dear Lord
To think You would use
A basket of trash
To teach me another lesson
On my slow walk toward maturity!

PROGRESSION

Dear Lord, it works
In continual progression.
The joy of the Lord
Is my strength.
And strength renewed
Brings added joy.
Beautiful discovery!

A MILLIONAIRE

Lord
Since I've begun to tithe my income
Giving You ten percent of my earnings—
Then going beyond my tithe
As a special love gift to You—
A wonderful thing has happened.
To my overwhelming amazement
You've made me a millionaire!
I don't mean in money, Lord
But in Big Beautiful Blessings.
The truth is, I'm so rich
I must constantly ask You
To advise me on new ways
To invest my incredible wealth.
Teach me to invest wisely, responsibly
For Your great honor, Lord
And for the continual enrichment
Of the Family of God.

DEDUCTION

Lord, when You say
The same thing to me so often
I surely must need it
And You surely must mean it!
Help me to take You seriously.
May I remember that the one settled proof
That I have taken you seriously
Will always be—obedience.

ECSTASY OF JOY

O dear God
What ecstasy of joy
That You took the whole of me
And made me wholly Yours!

I'M CONFUSED

Lord, I'm confused
About something:
You somehow seem
So extremely reluctant
To let me in
On Your plans for me
Very far in advance.
You assure me
Of only two things:
You are God
And You are good.

Little one
I leave nothing
You need to know
Unsaid.

TO KNOW GOD

O God
There is an aching longing within me
To know more and more
Of Your kindness and peace.
You have promised to give me
(As I learn to know You better)
Everything I could possibly need
For walking in newness of life.
By Your mighty power
You have promised to implant
Your own character within me.
But Your Word makes it clear, Lord
That to obtain these gifts
I need more than faith.
I must discover what You want me to do.
I must put aside my own desires
And strive to become patient and godly.
I must gladly let You have your way with me.
I must learn to enjoy and love others deeply.

You make it very clear, dear Lord
That the process is a build-up—
Addition upon addition.
But as I willingly yield to You
The reward will be the fulfillment
Of my deepest longing:
I will be spiritually strong
I will be fruitful and useful.
Above all, I will fulfill

Your divine purpose for my life.
For to know You, the eternal God
Is exactly what I was made for.

FRUITLESS HOURS

My Lord
Forgive me for spending
So many fruitless hours
Debating, analyzing, mulling over
What I think I should do
In future years—
When again and again
You have proven
That the hours of each *today*
Lived in explicit obedience
Reveal sufficient spiritual insight
To make *tomorrow* surprisingly clear.

Heartprints

THE REST OF THE WAY

He lay in his hospital bed
So weak he could scarcely move.
Slowly, quietly he told me
He had been meditating on the words
And Enoch walked with God.
Then he said serenely
"I'm walking with Him, too . . .
All the rest of the way."

FORGIVING LORD

Forgiving Lord
I long for her release—
My friend who churns
With memories of failure and guilt.
She needs to feel sure and serene
Knowing You are holding her fast.
She needs to understand
That her continual remorse
Is a sheer waste of energy and time.
In no way can she change the past
Or relive it
Or rectify it.
Lord, she is torturing herself
In her circle of regret.

Please speak to her, God.
May she no longer censure herself
For what once happened.
Rather, direct her attention
To what is happening now.
May she stop berating herself
For her mismanaged past.
Empower her to concentrate
On managing the present.
Heal her, Lord!
She is so occupied
With morbid introspection.
Give her a fresh, breathtaking glimpse
Of the joy that can be hers
When she is totally occupied with You.

HOW IS IT, LORD?

How is it, Lord?

My friend is able
To speak with amazing assurance
About Your sustaining comfort
In times of heart-throbbing grief.
She expounds magnificently
About Your shining presence
In times of fear and despair.
Her smiling declarations
About Your healing power
In the midst of tormenting pain
Are intended to encourage, I'm sure.
But I'm puzzled, Lord.
How can she speak so confidently
When she is so comfortably settled?
When she has never lost one
More precious than life to her?
When her greatest obstacle
Is her lack of discipline?
When by her own admission
She has never been sick
A day in her life?

O Lord . . . ever-patient Friend
Forgive me for the times
I have foolishly attempted
To offer the solace
That You alone can give.

GENTLE WHISPER

Lord
As I lie here in my hospital bed
Between clean white sheets
My heart swells with gratitude
That the small benign tumor
Is no longer a part of my body.
Vividly I remember
How You gently whispered, "Fear not"
The night before my surgery.

The pretty young woman
In the bed next to mine
Has just had her third surgery.
Her painful malignancy
Necessitates heavy sedation.
She has three children
All under ten years of age.
A year ago her husband left her—
Without warning or financial aid.
Lord, what did You whisper to her
The night before her surgery?

HEARTPRINTS

Whatever our hands touch—
We leave fingerprints!
On walls, on furniture
On doorknobs, dishes, books.
There's no escape.
As we touch we leave our identity.

O God, wherever I go today
Help me to leave *heartprints!*
Heartprints of compassion
Of understanding and love.
Heartprints of kindness
And genuine concern.
May my heart touch a lonely neighbor
Or a runaway daughter
Or an anxious mother
Or perhaps an aged grandfather.

Lord, send me out today
To leave heartprints.
And if someone should say
"I felt your touch,"
May that one sense Your love
Touching through me.

NEW REVELATION

O God
He did a superb thing for me—
This intellectual young lawyer
With his bold assertion
That You simply do not exist.
After three hours of intense discussion
After listening thoughtfully
To the reasoning of the human mind
I saw in a fresh and vital way
The immensity of the living God
And how tragic life would be without You.

A QUIET TONGUE

Lord, a revealing fact
Began to surface today:
I talk more than I listen.
I seem to be thoroughly convinced
That my ideas
My inspiring experiences
My bits of wisdom
Are exactly what all my friends need.
Too often I break into conversations
Confident that my enlightened insight
Will solve the predicament—
Whatever it is.
Obviously, I feel more comfortable
When I'm expounding.

But this morning at a Bible study
I cringed when I read Your command
In the first chapter of James:
"Don't ever forget
That it is best to listen much
Speak little, and not become angry."
At first I wanted to run.
But as the words kept battering away
At my guilty heart
I finally circled them with red ink.
Now, Lord, please help me to obey them.
Remind me daily, hourly
That listening is a discipline
And a discipline always costs.

I know I must pay a price.
The price for me
Is a listening ear
and a quiet tongue.

I SHALL GIVE THANKS

Dear God
I thank You that I have a share
In Paul's triumphant declaration:
"For me to live is Christ
And to die is gain."
So if it is Your wise and loving plan
To give me lengthy years
I shall give thanks
For added years to serve You.

And if it is Your wise and loving plan
To give me fewer years
I shall give thanks
For endless time to praise You.

FEAR NOT

Again and again, dear Lord
I read Your words, "Fear not."
Surely You would not say it so often
If there were any reason to fear.
Nor would You command it so explicitly
If You could not keep me from fearing.
God, You have given me a *Fear Not*
For every puzzling circumstance
For every possible emergency
For every trial and testing
Real or imagined.
Yet I confess wasted hours—
Even days, dear Lord
When fear clutches and clobbers me
Until I am physically and emotionally spent.
Lord, when David cried to You
You delivered him from all his fears.
On this gray-sky morning
I kneel before You with David's cry.
O my Father, I cannot believe
You would be less kind to me
Than You were to David.

GREATER UNDERSTANDING

O God
With greater understanding
My heart proclaims
Your own words:
"For my thoughts are not your thoughts
Neither are your ways my ways . . ."

What so often seems to me
An enormous trial
Crushing, mangling
Tearing me to shreds
Represents to You
An enormous transformation
Of my total self—
Purging, renewing
Liberating me
Until my soul soars!

DELIBERATELY STUPID

"OK," he said with an ugly sneer
"Explain God to me.
Does He have a nose and mouth?
Does He have long fingernails?
Where does He sleep—on a billowy cloud?
If He hears a million prayers a minute
How many ears does He have?
And why did He let your mother suffer?
Could He have prevented it?
If He's so loving and kind
Why didn't He heal her?
Yeah, and another thing:
Why doesn't He feed starving children
And strike His enemies dead?
Enemies like me, for instance."

(He laughed. He was very funny, he thought.)

I listened without responding verbally.
I knew whatever I said
Would only increase his rebellion
And feed his pride.
We'd been through this before—often.
As I quietly observed him—
His nervous gestures
The haughty tilt of his head—
I remembered what I had underlined
In Your Word just the day before:

86

"There are people who are
deliberately stupid and
always demand some unusual
interpretation . . ."

O God, it must break Your heart!

WASTED WORDS

I don't think I'm going to make it.
Maybe some people (like me)
Are just born fatties.
For seven tedious days I've been dieting
And I haven't lost a pound or an inch.

Listen, God
Please still my haunting conscience.
You know I'm just too sleepy
To count calories after midnight.
When I slowly edge my way out of bed
To tiptoe to the refrigerator
It's only to grab a very few bites
To tide me over until breakfast.
A small dish of ice cream—
Really very small . . . just a few bites.
Or a boiled ham sandwich
With thin, flimsy ham.
Yes, I know—
I did devour a stale doughnut
But I doubt that it counted.
A doughnut *that* stale
Just couldn't have calories.

In the morning I'll count calories again.
But listen, God
I'm deadly serious about my request.
Please still my conscience

Before I lose all my will power
And give up on the whole thing.

Dear undisciplined child
You might as well eat.
You're wasting words.

THE LESSON

Lord, for many months I prayed
To be filled with the Holy Spirit
That I might have more of Jesus.
But slowly You are teaching me
That to be filled with the Holy Spirit
Means that Jesus has all of me.

COUNT IT ALL JOY

Dear Lord
It is a comparatively simple thing
To face a group of hurting women
At a retreat or seminar
And share with them
The triumph that comes through suffering.
Over and over I proclaim from Your Word:
"Count it all joy."
I say it emphatically
And with genuine conviction.
But last month, dear God
When physical pain seemed unendurable
And my guarded emotions collapsed
All my carefully planned outlines
Crumbled like sand castles on a windy beach.
O God, forgive me! Forgive me!
Help me to recall often
The piercing words of Oswald Chambers:
"Our worth to God in public
Will always be determined
By our lives in private."
Teach me, dear Lord—teach ME
To count it all joy.
I have so much to learn.

SEND ME OUT

My Lord
Saturate me with gentleness
Stir me with deep compassion
Increase my spiritual vision
Then, dear Lord
Send me out into the world
With an understanding heart
To love . . . love . . . love!

THE MAJESTIC NAME

My hospital room
Is just a few feet from the elevator.
Third floor. Room 322.
Over and over I hear the monotonous hum
Of the sliding doors.
Open, shut . . . open, shut . . .

A white rubberized curtain separates me
From the fragile, gray-haired woman
In the bed next to mine.
I hear her frustrated sigh
As she constantly attempts
To find a comfortable position.
She is in obvious pain.

My own pain is so agonizing
My mind so steeped in darkness
I can neither read nor pray.
The smallest thing becomes a herculean
    effort—
Like pulling the sheet over my shoulder.
Like sipping water from a straw.
I feel helpless, just so utterly helpless.

But one thing I can do, dear Lord.
I can repeat the powerful Name of Jesus.
Again and again I say it:
Jesus . . .
Jesus . . .

Sometimes in a half-whisper
Sometimes in a muffled sob.

And You hear me every time.
Jesus, I *know* You hear me.
You answer by placing
Your everlasting Arms
Underneath my broken body.
You answer by Your gentle reminder
Of the pain You endured on the Cross for me.
You answer by renewing my assurance
Of Your everlasting love.

Jesus, there is a majestic sweetness
In Your regal Name.
Your Name is sweeter by far
Than the awful agony of my present pain.

NEW-BORN ECSTASY

When I resolve to come to You
Amid the chunks and cracks
Of all my mundane days—
When I resolve to listen
Really listen to Your gentle voice
Suddenly I know anew
That You are life
And life is joy!
Like a singing brook
Joy splashes over
All the common "dailies"
Until each empty space
Of my hungry heart
Is touched with new-born ecstasy.

HEAVENLY

Lord, You alone know
How many years
How many days and hours
There are between Now and Then
When I shall see You face to face.
But, Lord, as I walk with You
Day by day
Moment by moment
I'm trusting You
To make my on-going journey
From here to Heaven—heavenly!

SOMETHING BEAUTIFUL

Here I am, dear God
Your child
A member of Your Family
Asking You
To make something beautiful
Of my life.
Yet, even as I ask
I am convinced
That the one beautiful thing
About a child of God
Is You, Jesus Christ.
So, dear Lord
As You saturate me with Yourself
My life will be beautiful.

Life's
Journey

THE DREAM

"Darling . . .
Breakfast is ready."

"Please don't wake me up.
I'm having a beautiful dream—
It's about you."

O Lord
Breakfast can wait.
Sometimes dreams come true!

THE CROWN

God, through the years
Of our married life
You have been holding a crown
About ten feet above my husband's head.
He was simply too busy
Loving and serving to notice.
But I saw it.
Not only did I see it—
I watched him grow into it.

HIGH COST OF LIVING

Oh, how I ache for them, Lord
As they walk their separate ways
And yet continue to maintain
The same address.
What a lot of rent to pay
For a house so seldom lived in.
And what a lot of grief to endure
For a marriage so seldom worked at.

I WONDER

I wonder, dear Lord
Is my husband aware
When I set our small table—
When I serve him veal cutlets
Or chicken fried steak
Or sometimes an old-fashioned stew
Is he ever aware
(Between sips and bites)
That it's really my heart
I'm serving him?

STUPENDOUS TRUTH

Lord
In our marriage
You are teaching us
A stupendous truth:
We love each other more
As we love YOU
More than we love each other.

SEPTEMBER THIRD

September third.
Our wedding anniversary.

Lord, I wonder why *today*
I should suddenly remember
One of our first ridiculous quarrels.
It wasn't at all funny then
But I smile now when I recall
My stubborn resentment—
My blatant retort:
"I wish you'd go fly a kite!"

In one shining moment, God
You seemed to pour all the love
From all the corners of the world
Into my husband's gentle voice:
"I will," he said disarmingly
"If you'll fly it with me."

We've been flying together
For thirty-eight years!

CREATIVE CONFLICT

I still remember
My Aunt Martha's saintly advice
The day before our wedding.
With genuine sincerity she said
"God will be living in your home
So of course you must never quarrel.
Just pray, and everything will be fine!"

But through the years
It hasn't worked quite so neatly—
With or without prayer!
Nobody is in control
Every hour of every day.
Emotional levels vary.
The important issue
Is not whether or not we quarrel
But how we resolve our angers.

Lord, thank You for teaching us
To handle our conflicts creatively.
So many things which disturbed us
In our early marriage
Seem inconsequential now.
Thank You for the sunlight of forgiveness—
For the liberating words, "I'm sorry."
Thank You for reminding us
That learning to adjust
Takes years of mutual growth—
Growth stimulated by creative conflict.

CONFESSION

Lord
It suddenly occurs to me
That the most severe conflicts
In our marriage
Seem to come when I insist
On exposing my husband's faults
Instead of confessing my own.

FUTILE ATTEMPT

They are beginning the second year
Of their tempestuous marriage.
"We are miserable," they confessed
"And yet we really love each other."
Lord, help them to see
That their problem
Is not lack of love for each other
But lack of surrender to You.
They are demanding from each other
The infinite satisfaction
That You alone can give.
Dear God, somehow show them
That their marriage
Is in serious trouble
As long as they attempt
To be God to each other.

PRAYER FOR MY HUSBAND

Lord
I am impressed with Paul's statement
Regarding a Christian brother.
He said, "Then there is Apelles
A good man whom the Lord approves."

God, as these words lodge in my heart
They become my personal prayer
For him with whom I share my life.
In his challenging but strenuous work
In the arena of stress and strain
Please encourage and uphold him.
In moments of weakness
May he cry out for Your strength.
May antagonism give way to joy.
May he manifest sterling qualities
In the very thick of the battle.

Lord, I commit myself to this daily prayer
For the husband I have loved so totally
For so many beautiful years.
Continue to make him
A good man whom the Lord approves.

THERE ARE TIMES

There are times when we disagree—
My husband and I.
There are times when we frustrate each other
And say cutting things
So cutting that we're filled with remorse.
There are times when we criticize and
    analyze—
Times when we must hold each other tight
And ask each other's forgiveness.
But in all our years of marriage
Never are there times
When we don't love each other
With genuine, gigantic love.
Thank You, God
Oh, thank You for that!

LIFE'S DETOURS

O dear Lord
With all my heart
I thank You for a husband
Who can enjoy the scenery
Even when we must take
So many winding detours
In our life's journey.

QUESTION

Lord
I know I am mostly to blame
For our miserable quarrel this morning.
Self-assertiveness flared within
And my harsh accusations were unfair.
Here in the privacy of our kitchen
I can acknowledge my fault to You.
But why do I find it so difficult
To confess it aloud to my husband?

EILEEN

Eileen!
Even her name
Has the sound of music.

I miss her so much, Lord—
My beautiful friend
Whose entire life
Was a daily offering to God.
Now she is with You
Feasting on the inexpressible glory
Of Your majestic Presence.
O God, knowing her pure delight
In being with You forever
And knowing Your joy in having her there
Empower me to honor You
By yielding my heart's deep sorrow.
If need be, may I yield again and again
Until every hidden reservation
Is wrapped in love and trust.
O dear Lord
Though my eyes are full of tears
May my heart be full of praise!

TO RAINY

Lord, thank You for sisters—
Especially mine . . . Rainy!
Thank You for our gentle moments of sharing
Your love and goodness
In our individual lives.
Thank You for her concern, her kindness.
Lord, her beautiful sensitivity
And her dedicated talents
Are Your gifts to her. Thank You.
Thank You for creating fresh rainbows
Through blending her laughter and tears.
Thank You for giving her delightful days—
Days full of joyful surprises.
Thank You for giving her rugged days
To teach her that clouds are often chariots.
Thank You for her spiritual insight.
She is like a tree
Planted along a riverbank
Bearing luscious fruit
Each season of her life.

Deepen her faith, dear Lord.
Give her wisdom in all her decisions.
Give her spiritual discernment
And the rewards that come from being
Disciplined, obedient, consistent.
Thank You for her heart's yearning
To love You more dearly.

Though the miles separate us
Thank You that we continue to sing
Fresh melodies of love together.

I HOPE SO, TOO

He sat there in the corridor
Of the convalescent hospital
Trying desperately
To maneuver his wheelchair.
His bony fingers trembled.
A tattered slipper fell off his foot.

I asked if I might help him.
He nodded, and then began to weep.
For a brief moment I put my arms
Around his sagging shoulders.
Then I wheeled him down the narrow hall
To his small warm room.

He thanked me as best he could.
Then he added nervously
"I hope someday somebody will help you
Like you just helped me."

Lord, I hope so, too.

WHEN TROUBLE COMES

My Lord . . . my dear Lord
Again this morning
As I read the words of the Psalmist
You refreshed my heart
And replenished my hope:
"When trouble comes He is the place to go."

Trouble!
Always I am unnerved
By its unannounced entrance
Into the secret corridors of my soul.
Pushing through with frightening force
It comes in sinister shapes and sizes.
I am never prepared for its onslaught.

Trouble!
Fashioned as pain it overwhelms me.
As sorrow it grieves me.
As disappointment it numbs me.
As failure it defeats me.
As anxiety it entangles me
In a perilous net of depression.

But God
I have boldly underlined David's words:
"When trouble comes He is the place to go."
How foolish to go running
From friend to friend
From place to place

When You have promised to deliver me.
It is in Your proximity
That my frantic fears dissolve.

"When trouble comes He is the place to go."
In the margin of my Bible I have written
Yes!
Yes!
Yes!

LIFE'S PILGRIMAGE

Lord, I read in Your Word
That because of Calvary
You are bringing
Many sons to glory.
O God
In my life's pilgrimage
May I bring glory
To Your Son.

Other Living Books Best-sellers

THE ANGEL OF HIS PRESENCE by Grace Livingston Hill. This book captures the romance of John Wentworth Stanley and a beautiful young woman whose influence causes John to reevaluate his well-laid plans for the future. 07-0047 $2.95.

ANSWERS by Josh McDowell and Don Stewart. In a question-and-answer format, the authors tackle sixty-five of the most-asked questions about the Bible, God, Jesus Christ, miracles, other religions, and creation. 07-0021 $3.95.

THE BEST CHRISTMAS PAGEANT EVER by Barbara Robinson. A delightfully wild and funny story about what happens to a Christmas program when the "Horrible Herdman" brothers and sisters are miscast in the roles of the biblical Christmas story characters. 07-0137 $2.50.

BUILDING YOUR SELF-IMAGE by Josh McDowell. Here are practical answers to help you overcome your fears, anxieties, and lack of self-confidence. Learn how God's higher image of who you are can take root in your heart and mind. 07-1395 $3.95.

THE CHILD WITHIN by Mari Hanes. The author shares insights she gained from God's Word during her own pregnancy. She identifies areas of stress, offers concrete data about the birth process, and points to God's sure promises that he will "gently lead those that are with young." 07-0219 $2.95.

COME BEFORE WINTER AND SHARE MY HOPE by Charles R. Swindoll. A collection of brief vignettes offering hope and the assurance that adversity and despair are temporary setbacks we can overcome! 07-0477 $5.95.

DARE TO DISCIPLINE by James Dobson. A straightforward, plainly written discussion about building and maintaining parent/child relationships based upon love, respect, authority, and ultimate loyalty to God. 07-0522 $3.50.

DAVID AND BATHSHEBA by Roberta Kells Dorr. This novel combines solid biblical and historical research with suspenseful storytelling about men and women locked in the eternal struggle for power, governed by appetites they wrestle to control. 07-0618 $4.95.

FOR MEN ONLY edited by J. Allan Petersen. This book deals with topics of concern to every man: the business world, marriage, fathering, spiritual goals, and problems of living as a Christian in a secular world. 07-0892 $3.95.

FOR WOMEN ONLY by Evelyn and J. Allan Petersen. Balanced, entertaining, diversified treatment of all the aspects of womanhood. 07-0897 $4.95.

400 WAYS TO SAY I LOVE YOU by Alice Chapin. Perhaps the flame of love has almost died in your marriage. Maybe you have a good marriage that just needs a little "spark." Here is a book especially for the woman who wants to rekindle the flame of romance in her marriage; who wants creative, practical, useful ideas to show the man in her life that she cares. 07-0919 $2.95.

Other Living Books Best-sellers

GIVERS, TAKERS, AND OTHER KINDS OF LOVERS by Josh McDowell and Paul Lewis. This book bypasses vague generalities about love and sex and gets right to the basic questions: Whatever happened to sexual freedom? What's true love like? Do men respond differently than women? If you're looking for straight answers about God's plan for love and sexuality, this book was written for you. 07-1031 $2.95.

HINDS' FEET ON HIGH PLACES by Hannah Hurnard. A classic allegory of a journey toward faith that has sold more than a million copies! 07-1429 $3.95.

HOW TO BE HAPPY THOUGH MARRIED by Tim LaHaye. One of America's most successful marriage counselors gives practical, proven advice for marital happiness. 07-1499 $3.50.

JOHN, SON OF THUNDER by Ellen Gunderson Traylor. In this saga of adventure, romance, and discovery, travel with John—the disciple whom Jesus loved—down desert paths, through the courts of the Holy City, to the foot of the cross. Journey with him from his luxury as a privileged son of Israel to the bitter hardship of his exile on Patmos. 07-1903 $4.95.

LIFE IS TREMENDOUS! by Charlie "Tremendous" Jones. Believing that enthusiasm makes the difference, Jones shows how anyone can be happy, involved, relevant, productive, healthy, and secure in the midst of a high-pressure, commercialized society. 07-2184 $2.95.

LOOKING FOR LOVE IN ALL THE WRONG PLACES by Joe White. Using wisdom gained from many talks with young people, White steers teens in the right direction to find love and fulfillment in a personal relationship with God. 07-3825 $3.95.

LORD, COULD YOU HURRY A LITTLE? by Ruth Harms Calkin. These prayer-poems from the heart of a godly woman trace the inner workings of the heart, following the rhythms of the day and the seasons of the year with expectation and love. 07-3816 $2.95.

LORD, I KEEP RUNNING BACK TO YOU by Ruth Harms Calkin. In prayer-poems tinged with wonder, joy, humanness, and questioning, the author speaks for all of us who are groping and learning together what it means to be God's child. 07-3819 $3.50.

MORE THAN A CARPENTER by Josh McDowell. A hard-hitting book for people who are skeptical about Jesus' deity, his resurrection, and his claims on their lives. 07-4552 $2.95.

MOUNTAINS OF SPICES by Hannah Hurnard. Here is an allegory comparing the nine spices mentioned in the Song of Solomon to the nine fruits of the Spirit. A story of the glory of surrender by the author of *HINDS' FEET ON HIGH PLACES*. 07-4611 $3.95.

NOW IS YOUR TIME TO WIN by Dave Dean. In this true-life story, Dean shares how he locked into seven principles that enabled him to bounce back from failure to success. Read about successful men and women—from sports and entertainment celebrities to the ordinary people next door—and discover how you too can bounce back from failure to success! 07-4727 $2.95.

Other Living Books Best-sellers

THE POSITIVE POWER OF JESUS CHRIST by Norman Vincent Peale. All his life the author has been leading men and women to Jesus Christ. In this book he tells of his boyhood encounters with Jesus and of his spiritual growth as he attended seminary and began his world-renowned ministry. 07-4914 $4.50.

REASONS by Josh McDowell and Don Stewart. In a convenient question-and-answer format, the authors address many of the commonly asked questions about the Bible and evolution. 07-5287 $3.95.

ROCK by Bob Larson. A well-researched and penetrating look at today's rock music and rock performers, their lyrics, and their life-styles. 07-5686 $3.50.

THE STORY FROM THE BOOK. The full sweep of *The Book*'s content in abridged, chronological form, giving the reader the "big picture" of the Bible. 07-6677 $4.95.

SUCCESS: THE GLENN BLAND METHOD by Glenn Bland. The author shows how to set goals and make plans that really work. His ingredients of success include spiritual, financial, educational, and recreational balances. 07-6689 $3.50.

TELL ME AGAIN, LORD, I FORGET by Ruth Harms Calkin. You will easily identify with the author in this collection of prayer-poems about the challenges, peaks, and quiet moments of each day. 07-6990 $3.50.

THROUGH GATES OF SPLENDOR by Elisabeth Elliot. This unforgettable story of five men who braved the Auca Indians has become one of the most famous missionary books of all times. 07-7151 $3.95.

WAY BACK IN THE HILLS by James C. Hefley. The story of Hefley's colorful childhood in the Ozarks makes reflective reading for those who like a nostalgic journey into the past. 07-7821 $4.50.

WHAT WIVES WISH THEIR HUSBANDS KNEW ABOUT WOMEN by James Dobson. The best-selling author of *DARE TO DISCIPLINE* and *THE STRONG-WILLED CHILD* brings us this vital book that speaks to the unique emotional needs and aspirations of today's woman. An immensely practical, interesting guide. 07-7896 $3.50.

The books listed are available at your bookstore. If unavailable, send check with order to cover retail price plus $1.00 per book for postage and handling to:

Tyndale DMS
Box 80
Wheaton, Illinois 60189

Prices and availability subject to change without notice. Allow 4–6 weeks for delivery.

Other Living Books Bestsellers